Best Friend Bracelets

Friendship & paracord bracelet patterns

This edition published in 2018
By SpiceBox™
12171 Horseshoe Way
Richmond, BC
Canada V7A 4V4

First published in 2015
Copyright © **SpiceBox™** 2015

ISBN 10: 1-77132-358-2
ISBN 13: 978-1-77132-358-1

CEO & Publisher: Ben Lotfi
Editorial: Trisha Pope, Ania Jaraczewski
Creative Director: Garett Chan
Art Director: Christine Covert
Design & Layout: Kimberly Ang
Photography & Illustration: Charmaine Muzyka
Production: James Badger, Mell D'Clute
Sourcing: Janny Lam, Carmen Fung

For more SpiceBox products and information, visit our website:
www.spiceboxbooks.com

Manufactured in China

7 9 10 8 6

Contents

· · · · · · · · · ·

Introduction

. . . .

Friendship and paracord bracelets are a great way to share your fashion sense with friends! These fabulous accessories are easy to make, and you can pick any design and colors you want to express your style. Invite some friends over for a day of bracelet-making fun and then trade your creations with each other!

When you make a bracelet for someone, you can use their favorite colors or you can pick out colors that match their personality. Check out this list to see which colors would be perfect for your friend:

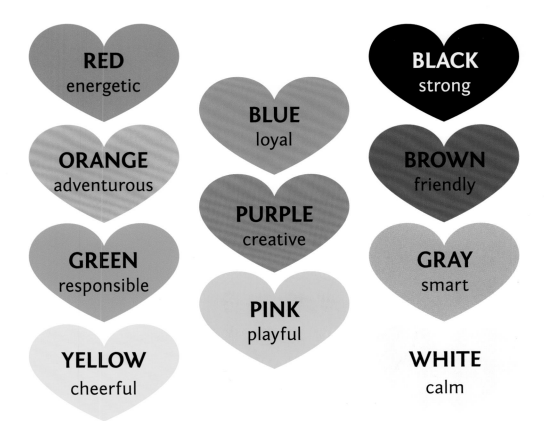

RED
energetic

BLUE
loyal

BLACK
strong

ORANGE
adventurous

PURPLE
creative

BROWN
friendly

GREEN
responsible

PINK
playful

GRAY
smart

YELLOW
cheerful

WHITE
calm

Friendship Bracelets

· · · · · · · · · ·

The next few pages will show you how to make friendship bracelets, both with the bracelet wheel and with the classic hand-knotting method. There is a great tradition that you can follow when you give a bracelet to a friend: Tell your friend to make a wish as you tie the bracelet onto their wrist. If your friend wears the bracelet until it's worn out and falls off their wrist by itself, the wish should come true!

Tools & Supplies

THREADS

It's best to use craft string or embroidery floss to make your bracelets. It's amazing how many different colors you can get, including glittery, neon and metallic threads! But you can make a friendship bracelet with any lightweight yarn or string that will hold a knot, and there are lots of fun yarns you can find in a craft or hobby store to experiment with. Remember that the thicker the threads, the chunkier the bracelet will be.

SAFETY PINS/TAPE

The easiest way to secure the traditional style of knotted bracelets while you are working is to tape the loose ends to your table or to pin the knot onto the leg of your jeans or to your bed.

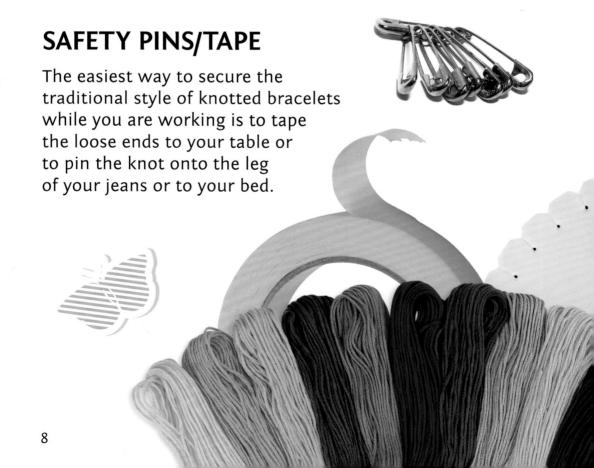

BEADS

Fun, colorful beads will make your bracelets even more eye-catching. See page 11 for tips on how to use beads in your bracelets. It's easy to do!

FRIENDSHIP BRACELET MAKER AND TEMPLATES

The friendship bracelet wheel comes in 3 pieces: the foam base, the pattern templates and the clear cover. The foam base is notched all the way around, has 4 small holes and one large one in the center. The holes in the templates need to line up with the holes in the wheel. Once they do, press the 4 knobs on the plastic cover into the holes to keep the template in place. Instructions for how to use the wheel are on pages 13–21.

Start
Départ

Awesome Stripes

Starting & Finishing Your Bracelets

· · · · · · · · · · ·

Each bracelet pattern shows you how long your threads should be and how many threads of each color you will need to cut. Once you've finished a bracelet, it's up to you whether you want to decorate it with braids, beads or anything else you can think of!

STARTING YOUR BRACELET

1. Choose the colors you want, then measure out and cut the number of strings shown at the beginning of the pattern.

2. Hold the strings together and tie the ends into a knot, leaving about 3 inches (7 cm) of loose string.

3. Follow the bracelet pattern until you have reached the length you measured out earlier (see next page).

4. To finish, tie another knot at the end of your bracelet. Leave about 3 inches (7 cm) of loose thread and trim the ends. You can also braid the ends for a cute look (see page 12).

BRACELET LENGTH

To make your bracelet the right length, measure your wrist with enough give so that the bracelet will be a bit loose. Then you can use the handy rulers on the pages at the back of the book to measure your work as you go. There's also a log to record the measurements of your wrist and your friends' wrists so you always know how long to make your bracelets.

ADDING BEADS

Inside your kit you'll find plenty of beads in lots of different colors. Here are a few ways to add beads to your bracelets.

1. When you finish off the ends of your bracelets, you can thread beads onto the loose strings and secure them with knots. This will give your bracelet a cute dangling charm effect.

2. If you are finishing with braids, tie a knot at the end of the braid, then thread all of the loose strings through a bead or two and tie another knot to secure the beads.

3. You can add beads in the middle of bracelets too. After a few rows of knotting, thread a bead or two onto the strings, bring the beads up against the last row of knots and then continue knotting according to the pattern. This is a great way to personalize the patterns and make them totally unique!

4. Finally, you can simply sew a few large beads onto one side of your finished bracelet. Ask an adult to help you with the needle and thread.

HOW TO MAKE A BRAID:

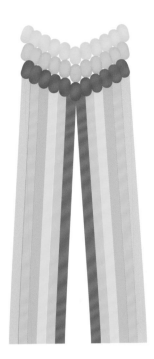

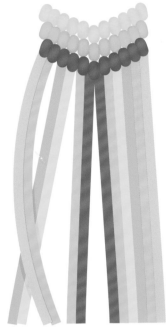

b   a   c

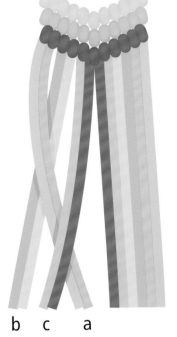

b   c   a

1. Split the threads in half down the middle. You will be making a braid with each set of threads.

2. Take one half of the threads and split them into 3 sections. Pick up the left group of threads (a) and move them between the other two groups (b and c).

3. Now take the right group of threads (c) and move them between the other two groups (a and b).

4. Continue braiding in this way, alternating between moving the left and right groups of threads into the middle, until you have about 2 inches (5 cm) of braid, then make a knot at the end. Make a braid with the other set of strings, then make 2 braids at the other end of your bracelet so that you have 4 braids that you can use to tie the bracelet around your wrist.

b   a

c

Friendship Bracelet Wheel

· · · · · · · · ·

The friendship bracelet wheel is a cool way to make fabulous friendship bracelets. You will want to make plenty of these bracelets to give to your whole circle of friends. They are going to love them!

There are 5 different pattern templates you can use with the wheels. Use the colors on the templates to start, and then once you get the hang of it, experiment with your own color combinations.

Setting Up the Bracelet Wheel

· · · · · · · · ·

PREPARING YOUR THREADS:

Look at your pattern template and select strings to match the colors on the tabs. For each color tab, you will need one string in that color. See page 10 for tips on how to get your threads ready for knotting.

 Scan this code to watch an online video on how to use the wheel!

Setting up the bracelet wheel properly is the first step. Whichever pattern you choose, you will need to set up the wheel the same way. Follow these steps carefully to get started.

1. Measure out and cut the number of strings you need, according to the materials list on page 16.

2. Set your wheel on the table with the START arrow positioned at the top.

3. Place your strings so that the knot is in the hole in the middle of the wheel, and the strings are fanned out so that you can pick them up easily.

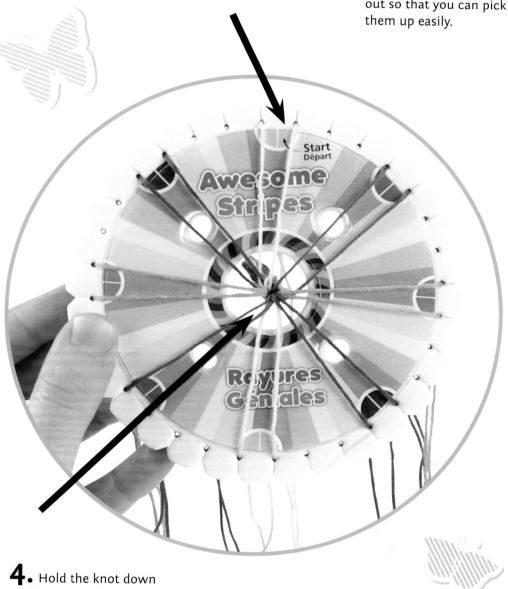

4. Hold the knot down in the center of the wheel with one finger so that it doesn't move, and with your other hand pick up a string and notch it into the wheel in a tab of the same color.

5. Continue to hold the knot in place while you position all of the strings into tabs of the matching color. Once they are all in place, pick up the wheel and adjust any strings that are loose. Your wheel is now set up and you can start making bracelets!

Awesome Stripes

Follow each step carefully for a few rounds.
Once you get the hang of it you'll see how
quick and easy it is to make these fab bracelets!

Materials:
4 colors: 4 yellow, 4 blue, 4 purple, 4 green (20 in/50 cm each)

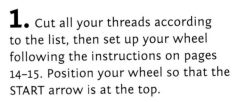

1. Cut all your threads according to the list, then set up your wheel following the instructions on pages 14–15. Position your wheel so that the START arrow is at the top.

2. There should be 2 yellow strings in the 2 notches at the top of your wheel and 2 at the bottom. Unhook the TOP RIGHT string from the wheel. Move the string to the bottom of the wheel, and hook it into the tab beside the BOTTOM RIGHT string.

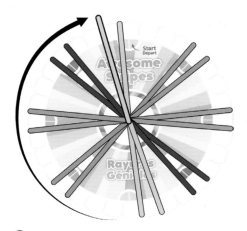

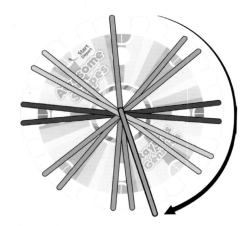

3. Unhook the BOTTOM LEFT string and rehook it into the notch to the left of the TOP LEFT string. Check to make sure your wheel now looks like the diagram.

4. Turn your wheel counterclockwise, or to the LEFT one tab. The BLUE strings should now be at the top of your wheel. Unhook the TOP RIGHT blue string and hook it back into the wheel beside the BOTTOM RIGHT string.

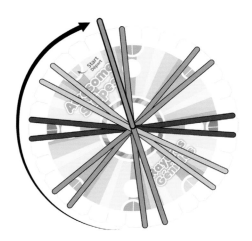

5. Unhook the BOTTOM LEFT string and rehook it to the left of the TOP LEFT string.

6. Turn the wheel to the left—counterclockwise—until the green strings are at the top. Continue hooking and rehooking your strings in the same way, then move on to the purple strings, and then back to yellow. Watch your bracelet grow!

TO FINISH: When your bracelet is long enough, unhook all the strings and tie them in a knot at the bottom. Trim the bracelet neatly, making sure you have enough thread to tie it onto your wrist.

Divine Diamond

2 colors: 12 green, 4 purple (20 in/50 cm each)

Follow the same instructions as for the Awesome Stripes bracelet. This time, however, your top 2 notches will have purple strings. To start, you will move the right string to the right of the green tab at the bottom of the wheel. You will then move the left string in the green tab to the left of the purple tab at the top.

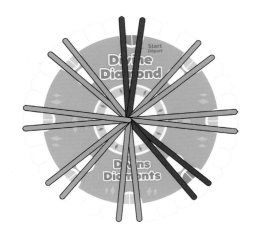

Lovely Hearts

2 colors: 6 yellow, 10 purple (20 in/50 cm each)

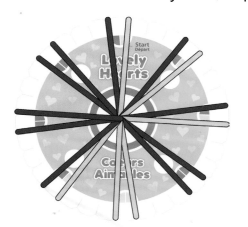

This bracelet is a bit different because some of the tabs have 2 different colors. But don't let this confuse you. Just follow exactly the same instructions for the Awesome Stripes and you will see a pretty bracelet of hearts emerge as you knot!

Fabulous Flower

3 colors: 1 yellow, 6 blue, 9 red (20 in/50 cm each)

The single yellow string creates the center of each flower. The 6 strings are the petals, and the remaining 9 strings make up the background color. After you have made this bracelet once to learn the pattern, choose your own colors and experiment to create different looks!

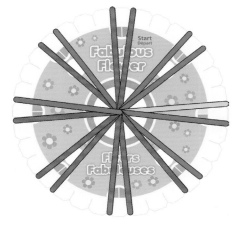

Keep in mind:

When taking a string from the top, take the thread from the right and place it on the bottom right. When taking a string from the bottom, take from the left and place on the top left.

Superb Stripes

This pattern is a bit different because there are fewer strings and tabs, and you are also not going to spin your wheel as you knot. Start your bracelet in the same way, by cutting and knotting your strings and then stringing them onto the wheel in the correct notches.

Materials:

2 colors: 4 pink, 8 green (20 in/50 cm each)

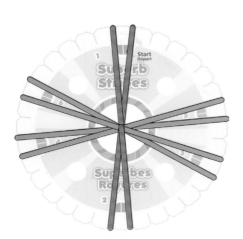 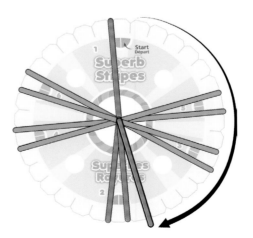

1. Unhook the TAB 1 right string and move it to the right of TAB 2.

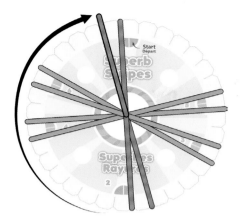

2. Unhook the left string of TAB 2 and rehook it to the left of TAB 1.

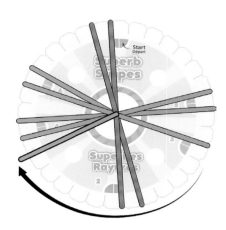

3. Unhook the TAB 3 lower string and move it below TAB 4.

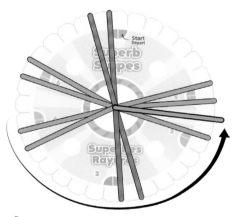

4. Unhook the topmost string of TAB 4 and rehook it above TAB 3.

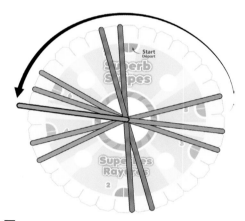

5. Unhook the TAB 5 lower string and move it below TAB 6.

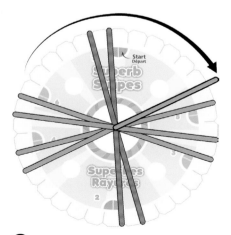

6. Unhook the topmost string of TAB 6 and rehook it above TAB 5.

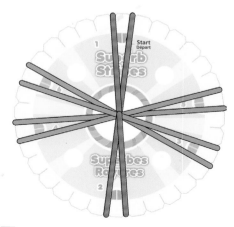

7. Move each string CLOCKWISE (to the RIGHT) so that they are lined up on the tabs again. Repeat steps 1–7 until you get the right length.

Classic Knotting

You don't need a wheel to make friendship bracelets. The next few patterns will show you some patterns for making great hand-knotted bracelets by using two simple knots.

A RIGHT-LOOP KNOT:

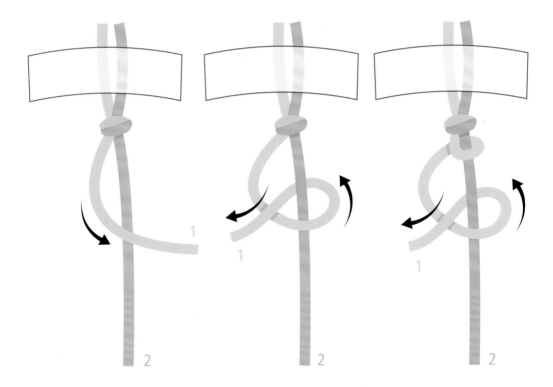

1. Knot 2 pieces of thread and tape them to a surface. Hold string 2 firmly and cross string 1 over it, leaving a loop like in the diagram.

2. Pass string 1 underneath string 2 and up through the loop. Slide the loop up to the top and pull it tight.

3. Now repeat the first 2 steps to make a double knot. You've made your first right-loop knot!

Tip:

After tying a **RIGHT-LOOP KNOT,** string 1 will lie on the RIGHT side of string 2.

After tying a **LEFT-LOOP KNOT,** string 1 will lie on the LEFT side of string 2.

A LEFT-LOOP KNOT:

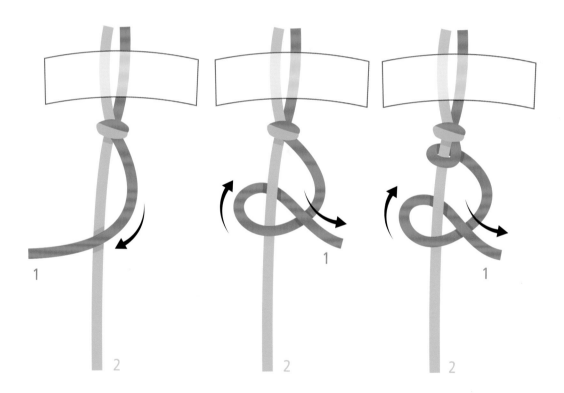

1. Knot 2 pieces of thread and tape them to a surface. Hold string 2 firmly and cross string 1 over it, leaving a loop like in the diagram.

2. Pass string 1 underneath string 2 and up through the loop. Slide the loop up to the top and pull it tight.

3. Now repeat the first 2 steps to make a double knot. You've made your first left-loop knot!

Simple Stripes

This is a great bracelet to start with because it only uses one type of knot that is repeated over and over. Once you get the hang of it, it's a snap to finish!

Materials:
6 colors: 1 string per color (28 in/70 cm each)

6 5 4 3 2 1

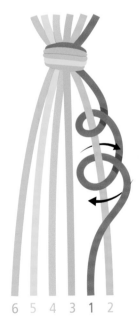

6 5 4 3 1 2

1. Tie your strings together and attach them to your work surface. To make it easier the first time, use the same colors of thread in the same order as in the diagram.

2. Pick up the string on the far right (string 1) and tie a left-loop knot over string 2 (see page 23). Pull the knot tight.

6 5 4 1 3 2

3. Still using string 1, tie a left-loop knot over string 3. Remember that you must tie 2 loops for a complete knot.

1 6 5 4 3 2

4. Next tie left-loop knots over strings 4, 5 and 6. String 1 should now be to the left of all the other strings.

1 6 5 4 2 3

5. Next pick up string 2, which is now the string on the far right. Tie a left-loop knot over string 3, remembering to tie a double knot.

2 1 6 5 4 3

6. With string 2, tie left-loop knots over strings 4, 5, 6 and 1. String 2 should now be to the left of all the other strings.

3 2 1 6 5 4

7. With string 3, tie left-loop knots over strings 4, 5, 6, 1 and 2. Continue this pattern with strings 5 and 6. When you have used all the different colors, string 1 will be on the far right again, and you can repeat the pattern starting at step 2 until your bracelet is the length you want.

Tie the loose ends into a knot, and your bracelet is ready to wear!

Cupid's Arrow

For this bracelet, you will take your knotting skills to the next level! Use the left-loop knot and the right-loop knot to make the V-shaped rows, or chevrons.

Materials:
3 colors: 2 strings per color (30 in/75 cm each)

1 2 3 4 5 6

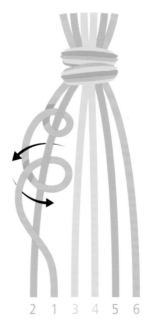

2 1 3 4 5 6

1. Choose 3 colors of thread and cut them into the lengths you need. Tie them in a knot and attach them to your work surface.

2. Start with string 1 and make a right-loop knot over string 2. Remember to make 2 loops for every knot.

2 3 1 4 5 6

3. With string 1, make a right-loop knot over string 3.

2 3 1 4 5 6

4. String 1 will now be in the middle.

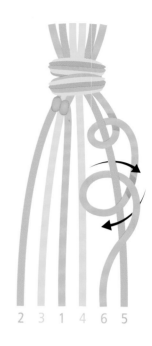

2 3 1 4 6 5

5. Now pick up string 6 and make a left-loop knot over string 5.

2 3 1 6 4 5

6. With string 6, make a left-loop knot over string 4. String 6 will now be beside string 1.

2 3 6 1 4 5

7. Take string 1 and make a right-loop knot over string 6.

2 3 6 1 4 5

8. You have completed your first chevron!

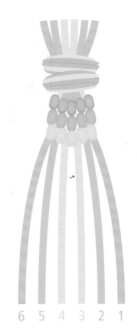

3 2 6 1 4 5   3 6 5 2 1 4   6 5 4 3 2 1

9. Now take string 2 and make right-loop knots over strings 3 and 6.

10. Take string 5 and make left-loop knots over strings 4 and 1. With string 2 make a right-loop knot over string 5.

11. Complete the third chevron the same way you made the first two. Now the colors will be back in the order they were in when you started.

12. Continue making rows of chevrons until the bracelet is as long as you want it to be. Finish it off and it's ready to wear!

Chevron Cuff

This bracelet is very similar to Cupid's Arrow, but is worked with four strings of each color to make it extra wide.

Materials:
4 colors: 4 strings per color (35 in/90 cm each)

1 2 3 4 5 6 7 8 9 10 11 12 13 14 15 16   2 1 3 4 5 6 7 8 9 10 11 12 13 14 15 16

1. Choose 4 colors of thread and cut them to the lengths you need. You should have 4 strings for each color you are using.

2. Take string 1 and make a right-loop knot over string 2. Remember to make 2 loops for every knot.

2 3 4 5 6 7 8 1 9 10 11 12 13 14 15 16

3. Continue making right-loop knots with string 1 over strings 3, 4, 5, 6, 7 and 8.

2 3 4 5 6 7 8 1 9 10 11 12 13 14 16 15

4. Take string 16 and make left-loop knots over strings 15, 14, 13, 12, 11, 10 and 9.

2 3 4 5 6 7 8 16 1 9 10 11 12 13 14 15

5. Take string 1 and make a right-loop knot over string 16 to complete your first chevron.

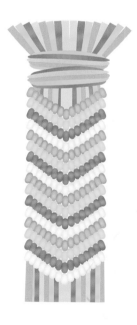

6. Make chevrons with each of the other colors the same way you did the first. Always start with the strings on the outside of the bracelet and work toward the middle. Continue the pattern until it's long enough to go around your wrist. Wear it with flair!

I Heart You

For this gorgeous bracelet, you will use the chevron technique you've already learned, but with a bit of a twist. This lovely heart pattern is perfect for Valentine's Day!

Materials:
2 colors: 4 strings per color (24 in/60 cm each)

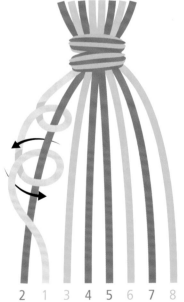

1   2   3   4   5   6   7   8   2   1   3   4   5   6   7   8

1. Choose 2 colors of thread and cut the strings to the lengths you need. Tie them in a knot and attach them to your work surface.

2. Start with string 1 and make a right-loop knot over string 2. Remember to make 2 loops for every knot. With string 1, make right-loop knots over strings 3 and 4.

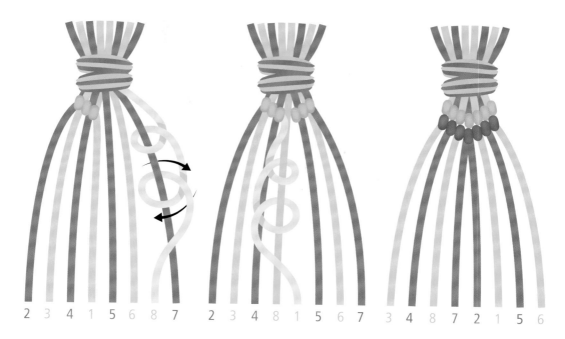

2 3 4 1 5 6 8 7   2 3 4 8 1 5 6 7   3 4 8 7 2 1 5 6

3. Now pick up string 8 and make left-loop knots over strings 7, 6 and 5.

4. Take string 1 and make a right-loop knot over string 8 to complete the first chevron.

5. Make a second chevron the same way, knotting with strings 2 and 7.

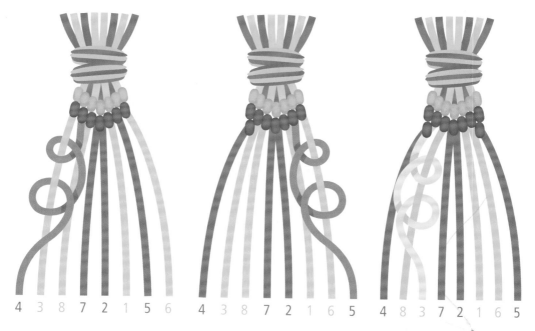

4 3 8 7 2 1 5 6   4 3 8 7 2 1 6 5   4 8 3 7 2 1 6 5

6. Go back to the left side of the bracelet, but skip the first string. Pick up string 4 and make a left-loop knot over string 3.

7. On the other side, take string 5 and make a right-loop knot over string 6.

8. Now you are going to begin your first heart! Take string 3 and make right-loop knots over strings 8 and 7.

33

4 8 7 3 6 2 1 5

9. With string 6, make left-loop knots over strings 1 and 2.

4 8 7 6 3 2 1 5

10. Take string 3 and make a right-loop knot over string 6.

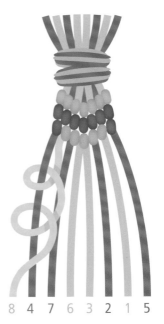

8 4 7 6 3 2 1 5

11. Again, skip the first string on the left and pick up string 8. Make a left-loop knot over string 4.

8 4 7 6 3 2 5 1

12. On the other side, make a right-loop knot with string 1 over string 5.

8 7 6 5 4 3 2 1

13. Now take string 4 and make right-loop knots over strings 7 and 6. Then take string 5 and make left-loop knots over strings 2 and 3. Make a right-loop knot with string 4 over string 5.

7 8 6 5 4 3 2 1

14. To finish your first heart, take string 8 and make right-loop knots over strings 7, 6 and 5. Take string 1 and make left-loop knots over strings 2, 3 and 4.

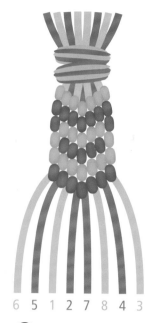

7 6 5 1 8 4 3 2

6 5 1 2 7 8 4 3

15. Take string 8 and make a right-loop knot over string 1. You've made a heart!

16. Make another chevron with strings 7 and 2.

17. Now you can repeat steps 6 to 16 until you have the length of bracelet that you want. Be sure to give it to someone special!

Diamond Weave

This is a more complicated bracelet to make, but with such a cool pattern it's worth the time and effort! Just keep your place in the pattern and keep knotting!

Materials:
3 colors: 2 or 4 strings per color—see diagram (33 in/85 cm each)

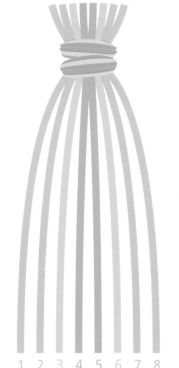

1 2 3 4 5 6 7 8

1. Choose 3 colors and cut them to the lengths you need. Tie them in a knot and attach them to your work surface. Arrange them as shown in the diagram.

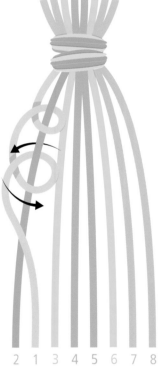

2 1 3 4 5 6 7 8

2. The first 4 rows of knots will be chevrons, as you made in Cupid's Arrow on page 28. Remember how this goes? Start with string 1 and tie right-loop knots over strings 2, 3 and 4.

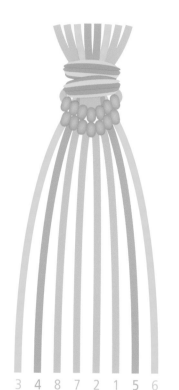

3 4 8 7 2 1 5 6

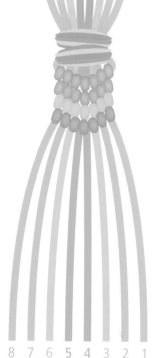

8 7 6 5 4 3 2 1

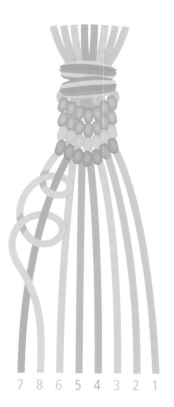

7 8 6 5 4 3 2 1

3. Then take string 8 and tie left-loop knots over strings 7, 6 and 5. Now take string 1 and tie a right-loop knot over string 8. Make a second row of the same color with strings 2 and 7.

4. Make a row with your second color using strings 3 and 6, and a row with the third color using strings 4 and 5. You should have 4 rows altogether, with strings 8 and 1 on the outside again.

5. Take string 8 and make a right-loop knot over string 7. On the other side of the bracelet, take string 1 and make a left-loop knot over string 2.

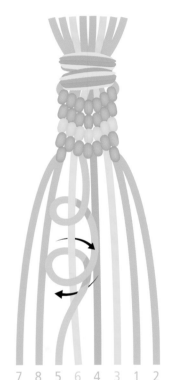

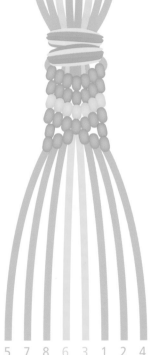

7 8 5 6 4 3 1 2

5 7 8 6 3 1 2 4

3 5 7 8 1 2 4 6

6. Now you are going to make the bottom half of the X. Take string 5 and make left-loop knots over strings 6, 8 and 7.

7. Take string 4 and make right-loop knots over strings 3, 1 and 2.

8. Now you are going to make an upside-down chevron. Take string 6 and make a right-loop knot over string 3. Now take string 3 and make left-loop knots over strings 8, 7 and 5. Then take string 6 and make right-loop knots over strings 1, 2 and 4.

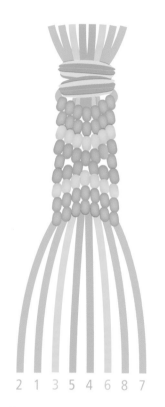

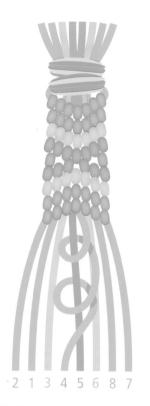

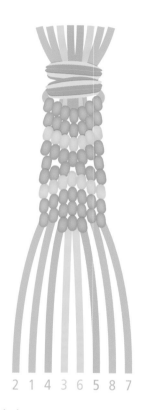

9. Make 2 more upside-down chevrons with strings 8 and 1, and strings 7 and 2, starting from the middle and working to the outside.

10. Take string 4 and make a left-loop knot over string 5.

11. Now take string 4 and make a left-loop knot over string 3. Then take string 5 and make a right-loop knot over string 6.

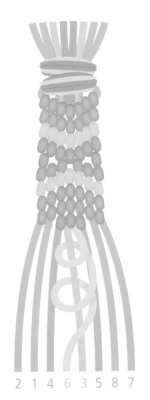

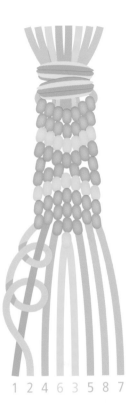

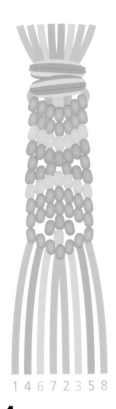

2 1 4 6 3 5 8 7

1 2 4 6 3 5 8 7

1 4 6 7 2 3 5 8

12. Take string 6 and make a left-loop knot over string 3.

13. Take string 2 and make right-loop knots over strings 1, 4 and 6.

14. Take string 7 and make left-loop knots over strings 8, 5 and 3. Take string 2 and make a right-loop knot over string 7 to finish the chevron.

To continue the bracelet, make another chevron in the same color, making knots with strings 1 and 8. Then repeat the pattern, starting at step 4. Note that the order of the colors will change in the next section. Look at the photo to see which color comes next.

Patchwork Stripes

For this bracelet, you won't be starting with the outside threads and moving in to the middle like before. Instead, you'll be knotting the threads in a zigzag pattern that creates a really exciting look!

Materials:
6 colors: 1 string per color (32 in/80 cm each)

1 2 3 4 5 6

1 2 3 4 6 5

1. Choose 6 colors of thread and cut the strings to the lengths you need. Tie them in a knot and attach them to your work surface.

2. Start with the second string from the right (string 5) and make a right-loop knot over string 6. Remember to make 2 loops for every knot.

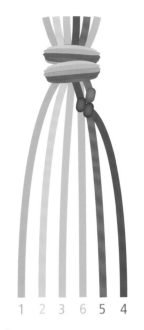

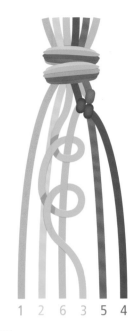

1 2 3 6 4 5

1 2 3 6 5 4

1 2 6 3 5 4

3. With string 4, make right-loop knots over strings 6 and 5.

4. You will see that the stripes look different from the other bracelets you have made.

5. Take string 3 and make right-loop knots over strings 6, 5 and 4.

1 2 6 5 4 3

1 6 5 4 3 2

6 5 4 3 2 1

6. Your bracelet will now look like this. Keep going!

7. With string 2, make right-loop knots over strings 6, 5, 4 and 3.

8. Take string 1 and make right-loop knots over strings 6, 5, 4, 3 and 2.

5 6 4 3 2 1

5 4 6 3 2 1

4 5 6 3 2 1

9. Now you are going to make stripes going in the other direction. Take string 5 and make a left-loop knot over string 6.

10. With string 4, make left-loop knots over strings 6 and 5.

11. You can see how the stripes are slanting the other way now. So cool!

1 2 3 4 5 6

12. Continue the pattern by making stripes with strings 3, 2 and 1. The order of the strings will go back to how it was at the start.

13. Repeat steps 2–12 until the bracelet is as long as you want it to be.

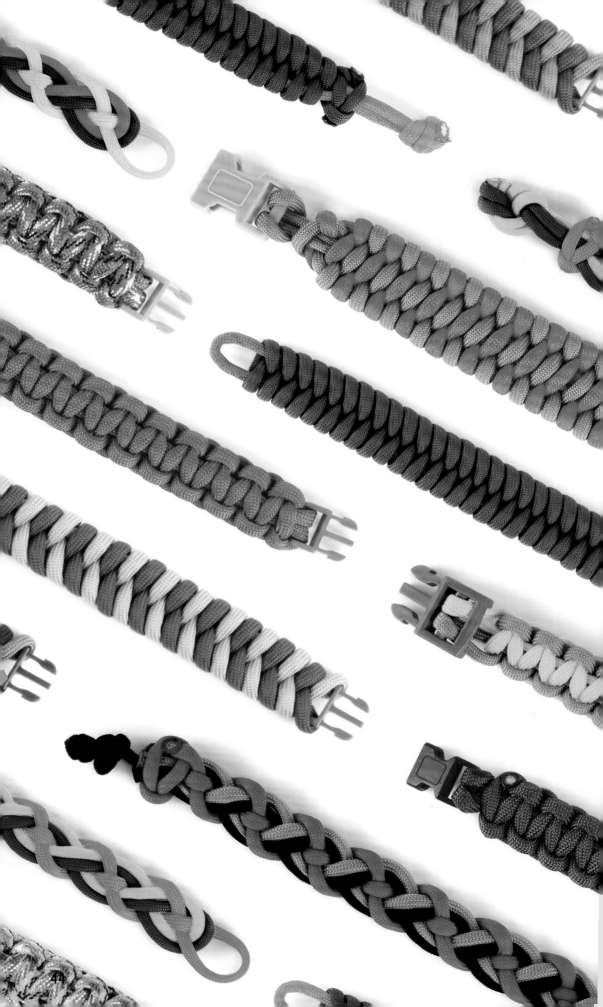

Paracord Bracelets

• • • • • • • • •

Paracord bracelets are simple and quick to make, and they look fantastic! Parachute cord is super strong and comes in tons of bright colors that you can mix and match to go with your outfits or the uniform of your favorite sports team. These cool bands are also called survival bracelets because, if you need to, you can unravel your bracelet into a few feet of cord that you can use in an emergency! Fashion has never been so awesome!

Bracelet Basics

HOW TO MEASURE OUT YOUR BRACELET LENGTH:

+1 in

1. Take a piece of cord and wrap it around your wrist. Pinch the cord where it meets the loose end.

2. Still pinching, line the cord up against a ruler and measure the length between the end of the cord and your fingertips. This is your wrist size.

3. Add one more inch (2.5 cm) to your wrist size to get your bracelet size, so your finished bracelet is not too tight. Example: If your wrist size is 5 inches (13 cm), your bracelet size will be 6 inches (15 cm).

How much cord to cut:

For most of the projects in this book you will need 1 foot of cord for every inch of your bracelet size. Example: If your bracelet size is 6 inches, you will need to cut about 6 feet of cord.

HOW TO JOIN CORDS:

For some of the projects in this book you will need to join two cords together to make one.

1. Take the end of one cord. Hold the end of the cord in one hand while you use your other hand to pull out about ½ inch (1.5 cm) of the fibers from inside. Cut the fibers off.

2. Next, harden one end of the other cord. There are two ways to do this: **A)** Put a bit of strong glue on the tip and let it dry. **B)** Ask an adult to melt the tip using a lighter.

3. Insert the hardened end into the other piece of cord that you hollowed out.

4. You can either use strong glue to hold the cords together, or ask an adult to melt them together using a lighter. Now you have one long piece of cord made up of two colors!

USING BUCKLES:

Buckles are a great-looking way to join the ends of your bracelets so you can wear them around your wrist. They are easy to use with paracord. There are two pieces to each buckle. One side has three prongs sticking out of it. This is called the hook end. The other side has a hollow inside. This is the catch end.

hook   catch   hook   catch

Horsetail Braid

This pattern will show you how to make a simple weave that you can repeat to make the entire bracelet. It's easy and quick!

Materials:
2 colors: 1 cord per color (5 feet/1.5 m each)

Figure out your wrist size (see page 46). For this design, you won't need to add an extra inch to the measurement to find your bracelet size.

 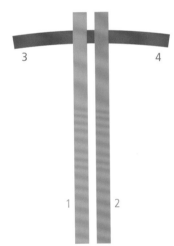 

1. Fold one of the cords in half and clip or tape it to a surface. Leave a ½-inch (1.5 cm) loop above the clip or tape. Leave the two tails of the cord hanging down. These will be cords 1 and 2.

2. Take the other cord and place it horizontally, with the middle under cords 1 and 2. Slide it right up to the top. The ends will be cords 3 and 4.

3. Take cord 3 and bring it over cord 1 and then under cord 2.

  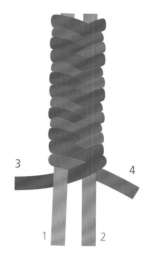

4. Take cord 4 and bring it over cords 2 and 3, then under cord 1. Push the loops you just made to the top of the bracelet.

5. Bring cord 4 over cord 1 and under cord 2. Bring cord 3 over cords 2 and 4, then under cord 1.

6. Repeat steps 3–5 until you reach your **wrist size**. Push the loops to the top of the bracelet as you go.

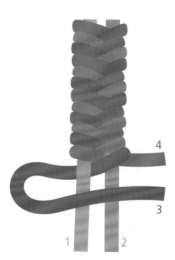  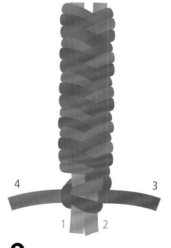

7. Take cord 3 and cross it over cords 1 and 2, making a loop on the left side.

8. Bring cord 4 over top of cord 3, under cords 1 and 2, and up through the loop on the left side. Pull the knot tight.

9. Take cord 3 and cross it over cords 1 and 2, leaving a loop on the far right side. Bring cord 4 over top of cord 3, under cords 1 and 2, and up through the loop. Pull very tight.

10. Trim cords 3 and 4 to ¼ inch (0.5 cm) and put glue on the ends to keep them from fraying. Leave an inch (2.5 cm) of cords 1 and 2 and then tie a knot. Trim the ends and put glue on the tips so they don't fray. Wrap the bracelet around your wrist and slide the knot through the loop to join the ends together.

Fishtail Braid

With this bracelet, you will join two colors of cord together so that you can create the striped look that you see. Then all you have to do is follow the simple weaving pattern to complete your bracelet!

Materials:
2 colors: 1 cord per color (5 feet/1.5 m each); 1 buckle

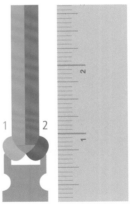

1. Measure your wrist and figure out your **bracelet size** (see page 46). Join the ends of your two colors of cord together (see page 47).

2. Thread the two loose ends of your cord through the catch end of your buckle. Slide the buckle down close to where the colors are joined, making a loop. Thread the loose ends through the loop and pull tight.

3. Now take the ends and thread them through the hook end of the buckle. Lay your cord and buckles against a ruler. The cords in between the hook and catch will be cords 1 and 2.

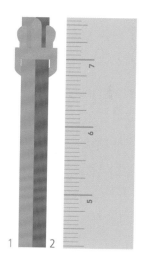

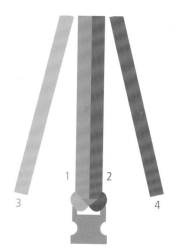

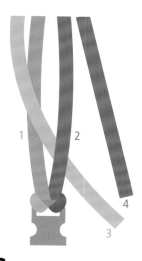

4. Adjust the hook end of the buckle until you get your bracelet size. Include the buckles in your measurement except for the three prongs of the hook end.

5. Clip or tape down both ends of the buckle so that the cords between them stay straight. The catch end of the buckle should be at the bottom.

6. The loose ends hanging down will be cords 3 and 4. Take cord 3 and bring it over cord 1 and under cord 2.

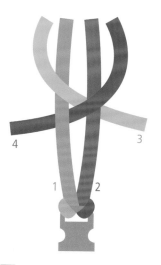

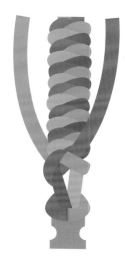

7. Take cord 4 and bring it over cords 2 and 3, then under cord 1. Push the loops you made up to the top of the bracelet.

8. Take cord 4 and bring it over cord 1 and under cord 2. Bring cord 3 over cords 4 and 2, then under cord 1.

9. Repeat steps 6–8 until you reach the other end of the buckle. Thread each cord up through a knot at the bottom of the bracelet and pull hard to tighten. Trim the ends to ¼ inch and dab glue on them.

Cobra

For the cobra bracelet you will use two different knots. Once you've got the hang of them, you'll see that this bracelet is a snap to finish, and it looks amazing!

Materials:

1 color: 1 cord measuring 1 foot (30 cm) for every inch (2.5 cm) of your bracelet size (see p. 46); 1 buckle

1. Clip the two ends of the buckle together. Fold the cord in half to find the middle. Thread the middle of the cord up through the catch end of the buckle, making a loop.

2. Take the two ends of the cord, slide them through the loop you created and pull tight.

3. Thread the ends through the hook end of the buckle.

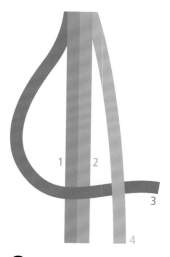

4. Unclip the buckles and place your bracelet flat against a ruler. Adjust the length until you get your **bracelet size**. Include the buckles in your measurement except for the three prongs of the hook end.

5. Clip or tape down the hook end of the buckle. Be careful not to slide the buckle around or your bracelet will not be the right size.

6. Take cord 3 and place it over cords 1 and 2, then under cord 4, making the letter "q."

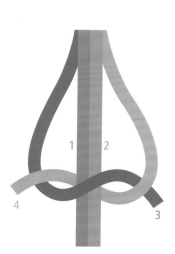

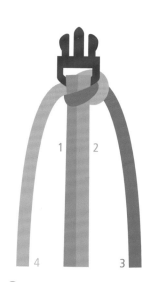

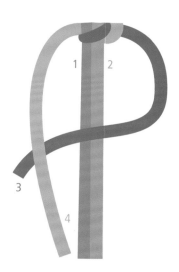

7. Take cord 4 and slide it under cords 1 and 2, then up through the loop created in step 6.

8. Pull on the strings to tighten the knot up near the buckle.

9. Take cord 3 and place it over cords 1 and 2, then under cord 4, making the letter "p."

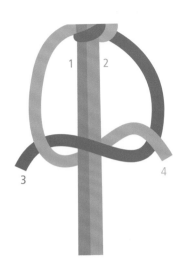

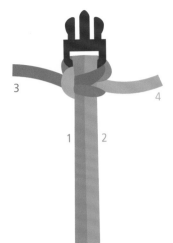

10. Take cord 4 and bring it over cord 3, then under cords 1 and 2 and up through the loop created in step 9.

11. Pull on the strings to tighten the knot.

12. Repeat steps 6–11 until you reach the catch end of the buckle.

13. Try your bracelet on to make sure it fits before trimming. If it fits, trim the ends to about ¼ inch (0.5 cm). Put some glue on the loose ends to keep them from fraying.

Celtic Knot

You will be working with more strings for this bracelet, so you'll have to really concentrate on each step. This stylish bracelet is worth the effort though!

Materials:
3 colors: 1 cord per color, 1 foot (30 cm) for every inch (2.5 cm) of your bracelet size each (see p. 46)

1. Line up your cords in a row. Wrap the middle of one cord around the other two cords, crossing it at the bottom.

2. Bring cords 4 and 5 down over cord 6. Bring cords 1 and 2 under cord 3 and over cords 4 and 5. You will have three cords on each side. Tighten. Loosen the top (yellow) cord to make a ½ inch (1.5 cm) loop at the top.

3. Clip or tape down the top loop. Bring cord 6 down over cords 1 and 2. You should now have four cords on the left side and two cords on the right side.

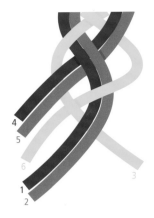

4. Bring cord 3 under cords 4 and 5, then over cord 6 so that it ends up on the right side. Pull to tighten.

5. Take cords 1 and 2 and bring them over cord 3. You should have five cords on the left side now and one cord on the right.

6. Take cords 4 and 5 and bring them under cord 6 and over cords 1 and 2, ending on the right side of the bracelet. You should have three cords on each side. Tighten.

7. The colors will now be in the same order as when you started. Repeat steps 3–6 until you have reached your **bracelet size** (see page 46).

8. Take cord 3 and cross it over cords 1, 2, 4 and 5, making a loop on the right.

9. Take cord 6 and bring it over cord 3 and under cords 1, 2, 4 and 5. Bring it through the loop you made in step 8. Pull to tighten.

10. Make a loop with cord 3, crossing it over the middle cords.

11. Bring cord 6 over cord 3, under the middle cords, then up through the loop you made in step 10.

12. Pull firmly on cords 3 and 6 to tighten.

13. Trim the ends of cords 3 and 6 to ¼ inch (0.5 cm) and put some glue on the tips.

Tie the other 4 cords into a double knot. Trim the ends of the cords, put some glue on the tips and let it dry. To wear your bracelet, wrap it around your wrist and slide the knot through the loop at the other end.

Ladder Rack

This bracelet is a trendy, extra thick wristband. The technique is a little bit different because you will be working from the bottom up. Follow the instructions closely so you can keep track of which step comes next.

Materials:
2 colors: 1 cord per color (5 feet/1.5 m each); 1 buckle

1. Join the two colors of cord (see page 47).

2. Fold the cord in half and slide the middle up through the catch end of the buckle, making a loop.

3. Take the ends and pull them through the loop. Pull tight.

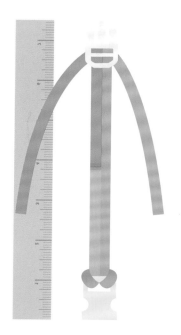

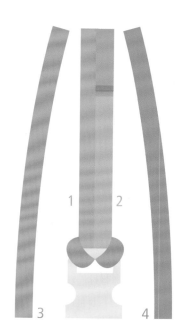

4. Now thread the ends of the cord through the hook end of the buckle, then unclip the buckle. Place the cords against a ruler and adjust the length until you get your bracelet size. Include the buckle in your measurement, except for the three prongs on the hook end.

5. Tape or clip down the hook end at the top and let the ends of the strings hang down. You might want to tape down the catch end too.

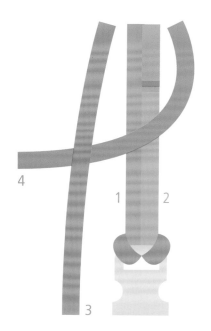

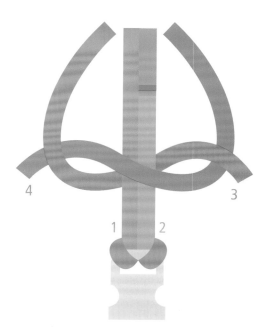

6. Take cord 4 and place it over cords 1 and 2, creating the letter "p."

7. Bring cord 3 over cord 4 and under cords 1 and 2. Thread it through the loop of the "p."

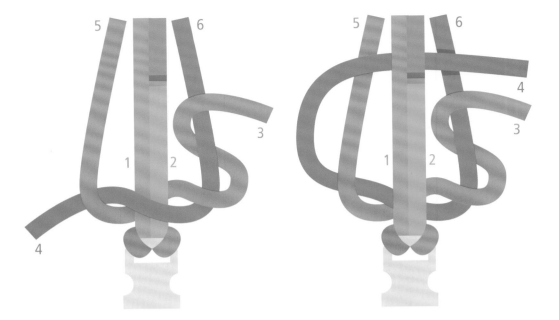

8. Move the knot down so that it is snug against the catch end of the buckle. Take cord 3 and wrap it once around cord 6.

9. Take cord 4 and place it over cord 5, under cords 1 and 2, and over cord 6. Tighten.

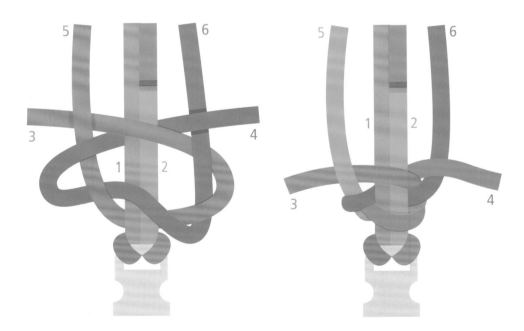

10. Take cord 3 and bring it over cords 1 and 2, then under cord 5.

11. Pull both cords to tighten.

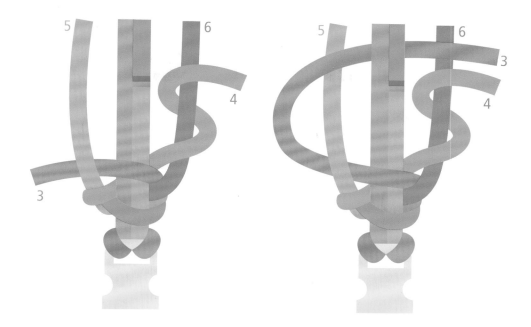

12. Take cord 4 and wrap it once around cord 6.

13. Take cord 3 and bring it over cord 5, under cords 1 and 2, then over cord 6. Pull tight.

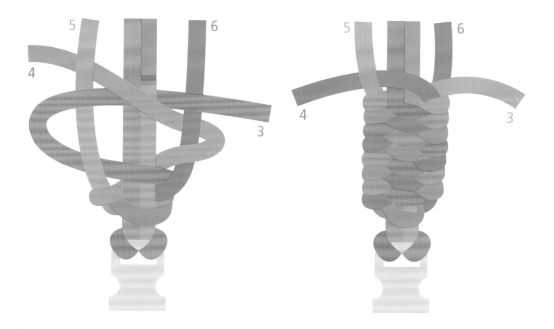

14. Take cord 4 and place it over cords 1 and 2, then under cord 5.

15. Repeat steps 8–14 until you reach the top. Always do step 8 using the cord on the right side. Trim the ends and glue the tips to keep them from fraying.

Friendship Bracelet Log

Bracelet: _____

Made by: _____

Given to: _____

Date: _____

Notes: _____

_____

_____

Bracelet: _____

Made by: _____

Given to: _____

Date: _____

Notes: _____

_____

_____

Bracelet: _____

Made by: _____

Given to: _____

Date: _____

Notes: _____

_____

_____

Bracelet: _____

Made by: _____

Given to: _____

Date: _____

Notes: _____

_____

_____

Bracelet: _____

Made by: _____

Given to: _____

Date: _____

Notes: _____

_____

_____

cm.

0

1

2

3

4

5

6

7

8

9

10

11

12

13

14

15

16

17

18

19

20

21

22

23

24

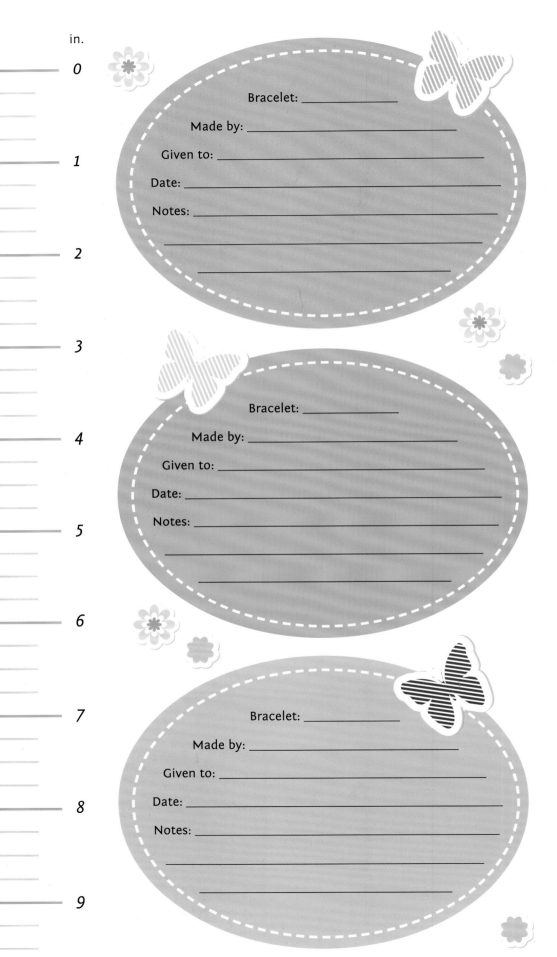

in.

0

1

2

3

4

5

6

7

8

9

Bracelet: _____

Made by: _____

Given to: _____

Date: _____

Notes: _____

_____

_____

Bracelet: _____

Made by: _____

Given to: _____

Date: _____

Notes: _____

_____

_____

Bracelet: _____

Made by: _____

Given to: _____

Date: _____

Notes: _____

_____

_____